'It's coming —
the postponeless
Creature . . .'

EMILY DICKINSON

Born 1830, Amherst, Massachusetts

Died 1886, Amherst, Massachusetts

This selection is taken from *Complete Poems*,
Martin Secker, 1933.

EMILY DICKINSON

My life had stood a loaded gun

PENGUIN BOOKS

PENGUIN CLASSICS

UK | USA | Canada | Ireland | Australia
India | New Zealand | South Africa

Penguin Classics is part of the Penguin Random House group of companies
whose addresses can be found at global.penguinrandomhouse.com.

This selection first published in Penguin Classics 2016
006

Set in 10/14.5 pt Baskerville 10 Pro
Typeset by Jouve (UK), Milton Keynes
Printed and bound in Great Britain by Clays Ltd, Elcograf S.p.A.

A CIP catalogue record for this book is available from the British Library

ISBN: 978-0-241-25140-9

www.greenpenguin.co.uk

MIX
Paper from
responsible sources
FSC® C018179

Penguin Random House is committed to a
sustainable future for our business, our readers
and our planet. This book is made from Forest
Stewardship Council® certified paper.

Contents

A wounded deer leaps highest,
I've heard the hunter tell;
'Tis but the ecstasy of death,
And then the brake is still.

The smitten rock that gushes,
The trampled steel that springs:
A cheek is always redder
Just where the hectic stings!

Mirth is the mail of anguish,
In which it caution arm,
Lest anybody spy the blood
And 'You're hurt' exclaim!

A precious, mouldering pleasure 'tis
To meet an antique book,
In just the dress his century wore;
A privilege, I think,

His venerable hand to take,
And warming in our own,
A passage back, or two, to make
To times when he was young.

His quaint opinions to inspect,
His knowledge to unfold
On what concerns our mutual mind,
The literature of old;

What interested scholars most,
What competitions ran
When Plato was a certainty,
And Sophocles a man;

When Sappho was a living girl,
And Beatrice wore
The gown that Dante deified.
Facts, centuries before,

He traverses familiar,
As one should come to town
And tell you all your dreams were true:
He lived where dreams were born.

His presence is enchantment,
You beg him not to go;
Old volumes shake their vellum heads
And tantalize, just so.

To fight aloud is very brave,
But gallanter, I know,
Who charge within the bosom,
The cavalry of woe.

Who win, and nations do not see,
Who fall, and none observe,
Whose dying eyes no country
Regards with patriot love.

We trust, in plumed procession,
For such the angels go,
Rank after rank, with even feet
And uniforms of snow.

The brain within its groove
Runs evenly and true;
But let a splinter swerve,
'Twere easier for you
To put the water back
When floods have slit the hills,
And scooped a turnpike for themselves,
And blotted out the mills!

I'm nobody! Who are you?
Are you nobody, too?
Then there's a pair of us — don't tell!
They'd banish us, you know.

How dreary to be somebody!
How public, like a frog
To tell your name the livelong day
To an admiring bog!

I can wade grief,
Whole pools of it, —
I'm used to that.
But the least push of joy
Breaks up my feet,
And I tip — drunken.
Let no pebble smile,
'Twas the new liquor, —
That was all!

Power is only pain,
Stranded, through discipline,
Till weights will hang.
Give balm to giants,
And they'll wilt, like men.
Give Himmaleh, —
They'll carry him!

I like to see it lap the miles,
And lick the valleys up,
And stop to feed itself at tanks;
And then, prodigious, step

Around a pile of mountains,
And, supercilious, peer
In shanties by the sides of roads;
And then a quarry pare

To fit its sides, and crawl between,
Complaining all the while
In horrid, hooting stanza;
Then chase itself down hill

And neigh like Boanerges;
Then, punctual as a star,
Stop — docile and omnipotent —
At its own stable door.

Is Heaven a physician?
  They say that He can heal;
But medicine posthumous
  Is unavailable.

Is Heaven an exchequer?
  They speak of what we owe;
But that negotiation
  I'm not a party to.

I took my power in my hand
And went against the world;
'Twas not so much as David had,
But I was twice as bold.

I aimed my pebble, but myself
Was all the one that fell.
Was it Goliath was too large,
Or only I too small?

Before I got my eye put out,
I liked as well to see
As other creatures that have eyes,
And know no other way.

But were it told to me, to-day,
That I might have the sky
For mine, I tell you that my heart
Would split, for size of me.

The meadows mine, the mountains mine, —
All forests, stintless stars,
As much of noon as I could take
Between my finite eyes.

The motions of the dipping birds,
The lightning's jointed road,
For mine to look at when I liked, —
The news would strike me dead!

So, safer, guess, with just my soul
Upon the window-pane
Where other creatures put their eyes,
Incautious of the sun.

Heart not so heavy as mine,
Wending late home,
As it passed my window
Whistled itself a tune, —

A careless snatch, a ballad,
A ditty of the street;
Yet to my irritated ear
An anodyne so sweet,

It was as if a bobolink,
Sauntering this way,
Carolled and mused and carolled,
Then bubbled slow away.

It was as if a chirping brook
Upon a toilsome way
Set bleeding feet to minuets
Without the knowing why.

To-morrow, night will come again,
Weary, perhaps, and sore.
Ah, bugle, by my window,
I pray you stroll once more!

I know that he exists
Somewhere, in silence.
He has hid his rare life
From our gross eyes.

'Tis in instant's play,
'Tis a fond ambush,
Just to make bliss
Earn her own surprise!

But should the play
Prove piercing earnest,
Should the glee glaze
In death's stiff stare,

Would not the fun
Look too expensive?
Would not the jest
Have crawled too far?

'Tis little I could care for pearls
 Who own the ample sea;
Or brooches, when the Emperor
 With rubies pelteth me;

Or gold, who am the Prince of Mines;
 Or diamonds, when I see
A diadem to fit a dome
 Continual crowning me.

I felt a cleavage in my mind
   As if my brain had split;
I tried to match it, seam by seam,
   But could not make them fit.

The thought behind I strove to join
   Unto the thought before,
But sequence ravelled out of reach
   Like balls upon a floor.

The reticent volcano keeps
   His never slumbering plan;
Confided are his projects pink
   To no precarious man.

If nature will not tell the tale
   Jehovah told to her,
Can human nature not survive
   Without a listener?

Admonished by her buckled lips
   Let every babbler be.
The only secret people keep
   Is Immortality.

One of the ones that Midas touched,
Who failed to touch us all,
Was that confiding prodigal,
The blissful oriole.

So drunk, he disavows it
With badinage divine;
So dazzling, we mistake him
For an alighting mine.

A pleader, a dissembler,
An epicure, a thief, —
Betimes an oratorio,
An ecstasy in chief;

The Jesuit of orchards,
He cheats as he enchants
Of an entire attar
For his decamping wants.

The splendor of a Burmah,
The meteor of birds,
Departing like a pageant
Of ballads and of bards.

I never thought that Jason sought
For any golden fleece;
But then I am a rural man,
With thoughts that make for peace.

But if there were a Jason,
Tradition suffer me
Behold his lost emolument
Upon the apple-tree.

I dreaded that first robin so,
But he is mastered now,
And I'm accustomed to him grown, —
He hurts a little, though.

I thought if I could only live
Till that first shout got by,
Not all pianos in the woods
Had power to mangle me.

I dared not meet the daffodils,
For fear their yellow gown
Would pierce me with a fashion
So foreign to my own.

I wished the grass would hurry,
So when 'twas time to see,
He'd be too tall, the tallest one
Could stretch to look at me.

I could not bear the bees should come,
I wished they'd stay away
In those dim countries where they go:
What word had they for me?

They're here, though; not a creature failed,
No blossom stayed away
In gentle deference to me,
The Queen of Calvary.

Each one salutes me as he goes,
And I my childish plumes
Lift, in bereaved acknowledgment
Of their unthinking drums.

A route of evanescence
With a revolving wheel;
A resonance of emerald,
A rush of cochineal;
And every blossom on the bush
Adjusts its tumbled head, —
The mail from Tunis, probably,
An easy morning's ride.

Who robbed the woods,
The trusting woods?
The unsuspecting trees
Brought out their burrs and mosses
His fantasy to please.
He scanned their trinkets, curious,
He grasped, he bore away.
What will the solemn hemlock,
What will the fir-tree say?

The leaves, like women, interchange
    Sagacious confidence;
Somewhat of nods, and somewhat of
    Portentous inference,

The parties in both cases
    Enjoining secrecy, —
Inviolable compact
    To notoriety.

It sounded as if the streets were running,
And then the streets stood still.
Eclipse was all we could see at the window,
And awe was all we could feel.

By and by the boldest stole out of his covert,
To see if time was there.
Nature was in her beryl apron,
Mixing fresher air.

The rat is the concisest tenant.
He pays no rent, —
Repudiates the obligation,
On schemes intent.

Balking our wit
To sound or circumvent,
Hate cannot harm
A foe so reticent.

Neither decree
Prohibits him,
Lawful as
Equilibrium.

Where ships of purple gently toss
On seas of daffodil,
Fantastic sailors mingle,
And then — the wharf is still.

Blazing in gold and quenching in purple,
Leaping like leopards to the sky,
Then at the feet of the old horizon
Laying her spotted face, to die;

Stooping as low as the kitchen window,
Touching the roof and tinting the barn,
Kissing her bonnet to the meadow, —
And the juggler of day is gone!

There is a word
    Which bears a sword
    Can pierce an armed man.
It hurls its barbed syllables, —
    At once is mute again.

But where it fell
The saved will tell
    On patriotic day,
Some epauletted brother
    Gave his breath away.

Wherever runs the breathless sun,
    Wherever roams the day,
There is its noiseless onset,
    There is its victory!
Behold the keenest marksman!
    The most accomplished shot!
Time's sublimest target
    Is a soul 'forgot'!

He fumbles at your spirit
  As players at the keys
Before they drop full music on;
  He stuns you by degrees,

Prepares your brittle substance
  For the ethereal blow,
By fainter hammers, further heard,
  Then nearer, then so slow

Your breath has time to straighten,
  Your brain to bubble cool, —
Deals one imperial thunderbolt
  That scalps your naked soul.

Because I could not stop for Death,
He kindly stopped for me;
The carriage held but just ourselves
And Immortality.

We slowly drove, he knew no haste,
And I had put away
My labor, and my leisure too,
For his civility.

We passed the school where children played
At wrestling in a ring;
We passed the fields of gazing grain,
We passed the setting sun.

We paused before a house that seemed
A swelling of the ground;
The roof was scarcely visible,
The cornice but a mound.

Since then 'tis centuries; but each
Feels shorter than the day
I first surmised the horses' heads
Were toward eternity.

Essential oils are wrung:
The attar from the rose
Is not expressed by suns alone,
It is the gift of screws.

The general rose decays;
But this, in lady's drawer,
Makes summer when the lady lies
In ceaseless rosemary.

Death is like the insect
　　Menacing the tree,
Competent to kill it,
　　But decoyed may be.

Bait it with the balsam,
　　Seek it with the knife,
Baffle, if it cost you
　　Everything in life.

Then, if it have burrowed
　　Out of reach of skill,
Ring the tree and leave it, —
　　'Tis the vermin's will.

Bereaved of all, I went abroad,
  No less bereaved to be
Upon a new peninsula, —
  The grave preceded me,

Obtained my lodgings ere myself,
  And when I sought my bed,
The grave it was, reposed upon
  The pillow for my head.

I waked, to find it first awake,
  I rose, — it followed me;
I tried to drop it in the crowd,
  To lose it in the sea,

In cups of artificial drowse
  To sleep its shape away, —
The grave was finished, but the spade
  Remained in memory.

I felt a funeral in my brain,
    And mourners, to and fro,
Kept treading, treading, till it seemed
    That sense was breaking through.

And when they all were seated,
    A service like a drum
Kept beating, beating, till I thought
    My mind was going numb.

And then I heard them lift a box,
    And creak across my soul
With those same boots of lead, again,
    Then space began to toll

As all the heavens were a bell,
    And Being but an ear,
And I and silence some strange race,
    Wrecked, solitary, here.

Fame is a fickle food
Upon a shifting plate,
Whose table once a Guest, but not
The second time, is set.

Whose crumbs the crows inspect,
And with ironic caw
Flap past it to the Farmer's corn;
Men eat of it and die.

My Wheel is in the dark, —
I cannot see a spoke,
Yet know its dripping feet
Go round and round.

My foot is on the tide —
An unfrequented road,
Yet have all roads
A 'clearing' at the end.

Some have resigned the loom,
Some in the busy tomb
Find quaint employ,
Some with new, stately feet
Pass royal through the gate,
Flinging the problem back at you and me.

Summer begins to have the look,
Peruser of enchanting Book
Reluctantly, but sure, perceives —
A gain upon the backward leaves.

Autumn begins to be inferred
By millinery of the cloud,
Or deeper color in the shawl
That wraps the everlasting hill.

The eye begins its avarice,
A meditation chastens speech,
Some Dyer of a distant tree
Resumes his gaudy industry.

Conclusion is the course of all,
Almost to be perennial,
And then elude stability
Recalls to immortality.

To-day or this noon
She dwelt so close,
I almost touched her;
Tonight she lies
Past neighborhood —
And bough and steeple —
Now past surmise.

The Bible is an antique volume
Written by faded men,
At the suggestion of Holy Spectres —
Subjects — Bethlehem —
Eden — the ancient Homestead —
Satan — the Brigadier,
Judas — the great Defaulter,
David — the Troubadour.
Sin — a distinguished Precipice
Others must resist,
Boys that 'believe'
Are very lonesome —
Other boys are 'lost'.
Had but the tale a warbling Teller
All the boys would come —
Orpheus' sermon captivated,
It did not condemn.

Candor, my tepid Friend,
Come not to play with me!
The Myrrhs and Mochas of the Mind
Are its Iniquity.

On my volcano grows the grass, —
A meditative spot,
An area for a bird to choose
Would be the general thought.

How red the fire reeks below,
How insecure the sod —
Did I disclose, would populate
With awe my solitude.

Color, Caste, Denomination —
These are Time's affair,
Death's division classifying
Does not know they are.

As in sleep — all here forgotten,
Tenets put behind,
Death's large democratic fingers
Rub away the brand.

If Circassian — He is careless —
If He put away
Chrysalis of Blonde or Umber,
Equal butterfly

They emerge from His obscuring;
What Death knows so well,
Our minuter intuitions
Deem incredible.

Doom is the House Without the Door —
'Tis entered from the sun,
And then the ladder's thrown away
Because escape is done.

'Tis varied by the dream
Of what they do outside,
When squirrels play and berries die —
And hundreds bow to God.

I dwell in Possibility,
A fairer house than Prose,
More numerous of windows,
Superior of doors.

Of chambers, as the cedars —
Impregnable of eye;
And for an everlasting roof
The gables of the sky.

Of visitors — the fairest —
For occupation — this —
The spreading wide my narrow hands
To gather Paradise.

To intercept his yellow plan
The sun does not allow
Caprices of the atmosphere;
And even when the snow

Heaves balls of specks like vicious boy
Directly in his eye,
Does not so much as turn his head —
Busy with majesty!

'Tis his to stimulate the earth,
And magnetize the sea,
And bind astronomy in place —
Yet any passer-by

Would deem Ourselves the busier,
As the minutest bee
That rides supports a thunder,
A bomb to justify!

(With a flower)
All the letters I can write
Are not fair as this,
Syllables of velvet,
Sentences of plush,
Depths of ruby, undrained,
Hid, lip, for thee —
Play it were a humming bird
And just sipped me!

It's coming — the postponeless Creature,
It gains the block and now it gains the door,
Chooses its latch from all the other fastenings,
Enters with a — 'You know me, Sir?'
Simple salute and certain recognition,
Bold — were it enemy — brief were it friend,
Dresses each house in crêpe and icicle,
And carries one out of it to God.

My life had stood a loaded gun
In corners, till a day
The owner passed — identified,
And carried me away.

And now we roam the sov'reign woods,
And now we hunt the doe —
And every time I speak for him
The mountains straight reply.

And do I smile, such cordial light
Upon the valley glow —
It is as a Vesuvian face
Had let its pleasure through.

And when at night, our good day done,
I guard my master's head,
'Tis better than the eider duck's
Deep pillow to have shared.

To foe of his I'm deadly foe,
None stir the second time
On whom I lay a yellow eye
Or an emphatic thumb.

Though I than he may longer live,
He longer must than I,
For I have but the art to kill —
Without the power to die.

Good morning, Midnight!
I'm coming home,
Day got tired of me —
How could I of him?

Sunshine was a sweet place,
I liked to stay —
But Morn didn't want me — now —
So good night, Day!

I can look, can't I?
When the East is red?
The hills have a way, then,
That puts the heart abroad.

You are not so fair, Midnight —
I chose Day,
But please take a little Girl
He turned away!

Longing is like the seed
That wrestles in the ground,
Believing if it intercede
It shall at length be found.

The hour and the zone
Each circumstance unknown,
What constancy must be achieved
Before it see the sun!

A toad can die of light!
    Deaths is the common right
  Of toads and men, —
Of earl and midge

The privilege.
    Why swagger then?
The gnat's supremacy
Is large as thine.